THE FEEL GOOD BOOK

1001 Ways to Be Happy

THE FEEL GOOD BOOK

1001 WAYS TO BE HAPPY

Bryan E. Robinson, Ph.D.
THOMAS NELSON PUBLISHERS
Nashville

Published in Nashville, Tennessee, by Thomas Nelson, Inc.

Library of Congress Cataloging-in-Publication Data

Robinson, Bryan E.
    The feel good book : 1001 ways to be happy / Bryan E. Robinson.
      p.   cm.
    ISBN 0-8407-3441-7
    1. Conduct of Life.   I. Title.
  BJ1581.2.R615   1992
  158'.1—dc20   92-29661
                                                        CIP

Printed in the United States of America

3   4   5   6   7   -   97   96   95   94   93

For Dennis Stabler
for the inspiration and courage
with which he has lived his life.

1001 WAYS TO BE HAPPY

1. Never put yourself last.

2. When you extend a helping hand to one person,
   be careful not to kick someone else in the teeth.

3. Always own a pair of old, faded jeans.

4. Count your blessings every day.

5. Acknowledge your successes along with your downfalls.

6. Burn the candle that has been in storage for the last two years.

7. Strive for progress, not perfection.

THE FEEL GOOD BOOK

8. Remember, the voice telling you that you cannot do something is always lying.

9. At least once a day sit and do nothing.

10. Don't close your heart so tightly against life's pain that you shut out life's blessings.

11. Celebrate all your birthdays no matter how old you get.

12. Examine your life for limitations and ask yourself why you put them there.

13. Plant a tree, pull weeds, or get your hands dirty.

~~~~~~

14. Diminish your wants instead of increasing your needs.

15. Cry when you feel like it.

16. Rejoice in other people's triumphs.

17. Don't wait for someone else to laugh or express joy.

18. Forgive yourself for any mistake you make,
    no matter how big or small.

19. Keep good company.

20. Never take a pill for a pain you need to feel.

THE FEEL GOOD BOOK

21. Use your enthusiasm to put yourself in forward gear and give yourself a spark to move ahead.

22. Look in the eyes of the ones you love when you are talking to them.

23. Remember that one is a whole number.

24. Walk in a summer rain shower without an umbrella.

25. Do a kind deed for someone else.

26. Keep your eyes and ears open to get the messages you need from people and events in your daily life.

1001 WAYS TO BE HAPPY

27. Be patient.

28. Eat something green.

29. Change what you can and leave the rest alone.

30. Walk hand and hand with truth.

31. Make laughter and joy a greater part of your life than anger and grief.

32. Embrace solitude instead of running from it.

33. Be zealous, not jealous.

THE FEEL GOOD BOOK

34. Forgive anyone you've been holding a grudge against.

35. Slow down and enjoy the present.

36. Walk in others' shoes before judging them.

37. Send yourself a kind message.

38. Remind yourself that the company you keep is a reflection of what you think of yourself.

39. Go on a picnic.

40. Accept your fears, no matter how crazy they seem.

1001 WAYS TO BE HAPPY

41. Don't let other people's opinions shape who you are.

42. Say a prayer.

43. Never attribute your accomplishments to luck or chance.

44. Know when to say *no*.

45. Look at the positive side of negative situations.

46. Remember that you are a spiritual being in a physical body.

47. Avoid seeking out other people for constant approval, because it makes them the master and you the slave.

THE FEEL GOOD BOOK

48. Go fly a kite.

49. Avoid fads and bandwagons.

50. Accept the things you cannot change.

51. Look inside instead of outside yourself
    for answers to life's problems.

52. Remember that *all* feelings are okay.

53. Shield yourself from bad influences.

54. Stand up for what you believe in.

55. Respect the wishes of others when they say no.

56. Seize every moment and live it fully.

57. Give away or sell anything you haven't used in the past five years.

58. Never downgrade yourself.

59. Take responsibility for what you think, feel, and do.

60. Pamper yourself.

61. Never say or do anything abusive to a child.

THE FEEL GOOD BOOK

62. Let yourself be God powered instead of flying solo.

63. Volunteer to help someone in need.

64. Refrain from overindulging in food, drink, and work.

65. Finish unfinished business.

66. Be spontaneous.

67. Find a constructive outlet for your anger.

68. Think about abundance instead of lack, because whatever you think about expands.

69. Think of yourself as a survivor, not a victim.

70. Cuddle an animal.

71. Be open to life.

72. See success as something you already have,
    not something you must attain.

73. Experience the splendor and awe of a sunset.

74. When you score a base hit, don't wish it were a home run.

75. Learn to be in the present moment.

THE FEEL GOOD BOOK

76. Instead of believing in miracles, depend on them.

77. Take a child to the circus.

78. Change your attitude and your whole life will change.

79. Never turn your power over to another person.

80. When your heart is at odds with your head, follow your heart.

81. Always remember that the past is gone forever
    and the future never comes.

82. Live your life according to what is right for you.

83. Acknowledge your imperfections.

84. Plant a seed and watch it grow.

85. See "friend" instead of "enemy" on the faces of strangers.

86. Watch an army of ants build their houses and cities and carry food ten times their weight.

87. Believe in something bigger than yourself.

88. Let the playful child within you come out.

89. Make haste slowly.

THE FEEL GOOD BOOK

90. Work through your problems step by step and one day at a time.

91. Accept compliments from others so you can see the truth about yourself.

92. Sit on the lawn without worrying about grass stains.

93. Don't condemn yourself for your imperfections.

94. Do a humility check periodically by loving the truth about yourself.

95. Tell someone you appreciate them.

96. Never live your life according to what is right for someone else.

97. Talk less and listen more.

98. Admit your wrongdoing and forgive yourself for it.

99. Thrive on inner peace instead of on crises.

100. Affirm all the good things about yourself.

101. Stop getting upset over things you cannot control.

102. Do the thing you like doing most, and do it often.

THE FEEL GOOD BOOK

103. Define yourself by who you are instead of by what you do.

104. Instead of complaining about what you need,
be grateful for all that you already have.

105. Make a list of all the people you have harmed and
be willing to make amends to them.

106. Don't take your anger out on innocent bystanders.

107. Remember to HALT when you are
Hungry, Angry, Lonely, or *Tired.*

108. Drink iced lemonade on warm, summer nights.

109. Let go of resistance and accept change.

110. Learn to *be* instead of *do*.

111. Let tomorrow take care of itself.

112. Take off your blinders, since you are not a horse, and look at the whole picture.

113. Find your uniqueness and treasure what is special about yourself.

114. Have the courage to be calm in the face of someone else's hysteria.

THE FEELGOOD BOOK

~~~~~~

115. Don't nitpick.

116. Remember that cleanliness is next to godliness.

117. Stop going back to the same people for the same rejections.

118. Don't take yourself too seriously.

119. Look at your life in a different way each new day.

120. Get the slogan right: "misery is optional," not "optimal."

121. Don't depend on other people for your
     self-esteem or happiness.

122. Have someone in your life you will always be there for.

123. Stop putting yourself down or calling yourself names.

124. Make sure you give at least one hug a day.

125. Make sure you get at least one hug a day.

126. Always have options.

127. Avoid clinging to and feeding off another person.

128. Buy wrapping paper when a child is selling it at your door for a school project.

THE FEEL GOOD BOOK

129. Make a good impression on yourself.

130. Admit all the things over which you are powerless.

131. Inventory your life daily and when you are wrong, promptly admit it.

132. Never assume you know what's best for someone else.

133. Treat yourself as if you are your own best friend.

134. Use your power and authority gently and with love.

135. Don't hire people because they're workaholics.

136. Learn to love others without putting conditions on them.

137. Remember that negative thoughts are prison bars on a self-imposed confinement.

138. Live by the motto that an ending is really just a beginning in disguise.

139. Be content with the moment.

140. Look at life as a course and your errors are lessons that you are learning in its curriculum.

141. Choose your life's work based on what you love to do.

THE FEEL GOOD BOOK

142. When someone asks you what you want, tell them.

143. Remember children bring *us* up, instead of the other way around.

144. Remind yourself that important things take time.

145. Don't let other people's negativity pull you down.

146. Do *small* things with *great* love and you'll make a *big* difference.

147. Always keep a good book by your bedside.

148. When life gives you roadblocks, take healthy detours.

149. Live by the daily reminder that no one can walk over you if you're not lying down.

150. Remind yourself that falling down is part of moving forward.

151. When things are at their worst, remember "this too shall pass."

152. Fill your life with joy.

153. Don't take on other people's problems. It robs them of a chance to grow.

154. Buy yourself a stuffed animal, no matter what your age.

THE FEEL GOOD BOOK

155. Improve your conscious contact with God through prayer and meditation.

156. Empower yourself without overpowering others.

157. Invite friends over even though the carpet is stained and the sofa is faded.

158. Wade knee-deep in water.

159. Learn to delegate.

160. Put something that has life in your house, such as plants or pets.

1001 WAYS TO BE HAPPY

161. Have faith in something larger than life.

162. Live today as if there were no tomorrow.

163. Put an end to speed-reading, quick-fixing, rush-houring, fast-tracking, and hustling and bustling yourself to death.

164. Find at least one thing that you can let go.

165. Tell the most important people in your life that you appreciate them.

166. Practice some belief, philosophy, or religion in all your daily affairs.

THE FEEL GOOD BOOK

167. Sit by a crackling fire and listen to soft music.

168. Tell yourself that you appreciate you.

169. Stop making excuses.

170. Eliminate the words *should*, *must*, and *ought* from your vocabulary.

171. Have dinner without television and with candlelight at least once a week.

172. Learn to *be* the right person instead of trying to *find* the right person.

173. Bring someone fresh flowers.

174. Want what you have instead of trying to have what you want.

175. Accept that you are powerless over what other people think, feel, and do.

176. Finish whatever is undone, but take your time completing it.

177. Exercise your power to choose what *you* will think, feel, and do.

178. Take another point of view, practice compassion, and get your mind off your own ego.

THE FEEL GOOD BOOK

179. Know when to call it quits.

180. Stop trying to figure everything out and follow your heart instead of your head.

181. Exercise.

182. Keep it simple.

183. Walk softly through your life with gentle power that will leave a large footprint.

184. Create your own unique life as you would weave silk through fabric.

185. Say what's bothering you instead of getting angry
when others can't read your mind.

186. Lie on your back in a grassy knoll on a starry summer night.

187. Stop trying to squeeze 48 hours into 24.

188. Live your life on nature's time schedule.

189. Develop your own values and beliefs instead of mimicking
the thoughts and opinions of others.

190. Flow with the river in the direction it is going,
instead of pushing against the current.

THE FEEL GOOD BOOK

191. Tell someone you love them while you still have the chance.

192. Ask forgiveness of all the people you have hurt through hurry and neglect.

193. Remind yourself that making a mistake doesn't make *you* a mistake.

194. Sit on the seashore and listen to the surf pound the shore and feel the mist kiss your face.

195. Look for God everywhere: in the trees, in the sunset, in birds' twitterings, in the gurgles of a baby, and in your emotions as you experience all these things.

1001 WAYS TO BE HAPPY

196. Mend a relationship while you still have the chance.

197. Do unto others as you would have them do unto you.

198. Let go of unrealistic expectations and accept the fact that nobody bakes bread or drives a car the same way you do.

199. Lie in a hammock, look at the treetops, and listen to the leaves brush against each other.

200. Remind yourself that self-hatred is a vagrant thought without visible means of support.

201. Play peek-a-boo with a baby.

THE FEEL GOOD BOOK

202. Make a confession while you still have the chance.

203. Distinguish between the changeable and unchangeable and you will achieve a high level of serenity and inner peace.

204. Don't become so accustomed to rearranging the truth that you believe the falsehoods you tell.

205. Be more than your work, your community image, or your material things.

206. Take time for yourself at least once a day.

207. Don't cling to the ones you love or you'll lose them.

1001 WAYS TO BE HAPPY

208. Remind yourself of what is most important in your life and be grateful for it.

209. Use your worrying energy for things you can change, and you will make those changes as the day unfolds.

210. Spend meaningful time with your kids.

211. Make sure your thoughts free you instead of bind you.

212. Step aside when you feel caught in other people's quarrels.

213. Keep yourself anchored with God so you won't be swayed from your spiritual path by the pull of life's ups and downs.

THE FEEL GOOD BOOK

214. Open yourself to change instead of trying
to keep things as they are.

215. Refuse to hang around and listen
to people gripe and complain.

216. Don't agonize, organize.

217. Rethink your plan of action when things
get too complicated.

218. Live by the motto that "change is the only guarantee in life."

219. Never let sleeping dogs lie.

1001 WAYS TO BE HAPPY

220. Surround yourself with people who love, affirm, and bring out the best in you.

221. Get in the spiritual flow instead of the cash flow.

222. When you fly off the handle, grab your anger by the tail.

223. Be willing to learn new things.

224. Look in the mirror and tell yourself that you love you just the way you are.

225. Decide that everything you do from now on will be by choice, not coercion or obligation.

THE FEEL GOOD BOOK

226. Notice what you are thinking at this moment and ask yourself, "Is this the way I want to live my life?"

227. Send out love and positive energy and it will all come back to you.

228. Stop waiting for someone else to make decisions for you and make them yourself.

229. Be willing to admit that you don't know the answer to a question.

230. If you have to choose between cleaning a closet and balancing your checkbook, go watch the sunset.

1001 WAYS TO BE HAPPY

231. Don't allow yourself to be put in the middle of other people's arguments. They need to work out their differences themselves.

232. Use your mind to free yourself instead of enslave yourself.

233. Be a big tipper.

234. Don't be afraid to look silly, laugh at yourself, and have a good time.

235. Be part of the solution, instead of part of the problem.

236. Please don't smoke.

THE FEEL GOOD BOOK

237. Remove the mask that you wear and share the real you with at least one person.

238. Always keep a pair of dirty sneakers around.

239. Take the energy you put into forming self-righteous attitudes and put it to good use on yourself.

240. Give yourself credit where credit is due.

241. Be willing to give and take as long as you're not always doing one more than the other.

242. Never allow shame and guilt to be used against you.

1001 WAYS TO BE HAPPY

243. Create within yourself a mental sanctuary where you can go anytime and find stillness and calm, become recharged, and find solutions to life's problems.

244. When you enter a rose garden, look for the roses instead of the thorns.

245. Do something romantic for the one you love.

246. Keep your feet planted firmly on the ground and your eyes toward the heavens.

247. Stop trying to make trees fly and to fit a size 9 foot into a size 7 shoe.

THE FEELGOOD BOOK

248. Put yourself in unison with life's perfect order.

249. Don't be afraid to rock the boat once in awhile.

250. Refuse to allow your life to be dominated by pessimism.

251. Create a world of impending optimism.

252. Get acquainted with yourself.

253. Make your mark in life through human virtue,
because material gain has no lasting value.

254. Think one positive thought a day.

1001 WAYS TO BE HAPPY

255. Drive to work in a thunderstorm as enthusiastically as you would on a sunny day.

256. Take chances where no physical risks to you or someone else are involved.

257. Feel your own feelings instead of someone else's.

258. Avoid relationships with people who put you down or minimize your worth.

259. Get some dirt under your fingernails.

260. Go barefoot.

THE FEELGOOD BOOK

261. Make up your mind about what you want in life, go for it, and don't let anyone stand in your way.

262. Walk instead of driving.

263. Skip instead of walking.

264. Welcome viewpoints that challenge yours.
They are an open door to a new way of life.

265. Be a peacemaker without compromising yourself.

266. When someone is lost and needs information, take the time to point them in the right direction.

1001 WAYS TO BE HAPPY

267. Try not to bite off more than you can chew.

268. Be yourself.

269. Find one person in your life that you can talk to in a time of need.

270. Be a teacher of life to someone.

271. Take care of yourself.

272. Accept whatever life delivers.

273. Express your opinion.

THE FEEL GOOD BOOK

274. Remember that life is a process, not an event.

275. Avoid wallowing in self-pity.

276. Feel mud between your toes.

277. Hang a set of wind chimes where you can hear them sing.

278. Compliment someone on how they look or what they do.

279. Try not to make keeping secrets a habit.

280. Make sure that when you aspire to a better way of life you are not aspiring to someone else's life.

281. Remind yourself that you deserve the best of everything.

282. Take time to contemplate the cosmos.

283. When you don't have time to wash your hair, wear a hat.

284. Exercise your power to choose your thoughts, feelings, and actions, no matter how hopeless your life seems at the moment.

285. When you procrastinate, ask yourself what you're afraid of not doing perfectly.

286. Eat yogurt instead of ice cream.

THE FEEL GOOD BOOK

287. Think about the things you love or hate in other people because they reflect something you love or hate about yourself.

288. Never fool yourself into believing you have arrived.

289. Turn obstacles on your path into stepping stones.

290. Waste time once in a while.

291. Make sure you know your neighbors.

292. Find one area in your life where you can substitute flexibility for rigidity.

293. Play Monopoly instead of video games.

294. Don't judge what's in someone's heart by the way they look.

295. Think in terms of shades of gray instead of black and white.

296. Whistle.

297. Choose happiness or it will not choose you.

298. Remember that nobody can make you feel anything.

299. Open yourself to new ideas and
     different ways of doing things.

THE FEEL GOOD BOOK

300. Take a different route home from work.

301. Make sure you learn the lesson in each of your mistakes.

302. Love your body, including your love handles.

303. Expect the best from life and that's what you'll get.

304. Smell the sweet breath of a baby.

305. Learn to relax.

306. Remind yourself that it's not what you say but what you do that counts.

307. Go out of your way to be hospitable on your turf.

308. Be a good winner and loser.

309. Keep a daily journal.

310. Support your local schools.

311. Work to live instead of live to work.

312. Learn to love yourself.

313. Avoid trying to read someone's mind.
Ask them to clarify what they mean.

THE FEEL GOOD BOOK

314. Easy does it.

315. Let someone else go first for a change.

316. Take up for yourself when your thoughts want to beat you up.

317. Know where to draw the line.

318. Clear your mind of clutter.

319. Sweat.

320. Learn to accept the people in your life *exactly* as they are without any *expectations* for them to change.

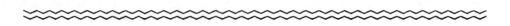

321. Never drink and drive.

322. Be sensitive to other people's boundaries.

323. Never give up on your dreams.

324. Let go of resentments.

325. Wait without tapping your foot.

326. Have a family of choice in addition to a family of origin.

327. Accept the difficult times along with the easy ones and you will get through them all.

THE FEEL GOOD BOOK

328. Be active in at least one community organization.

329. Drink water; it's free and filling.

330. Wherever you go, leave it better than you found it.

331. Think uplifting thoughts.

332. Never use sweets to reward yourself.

333. Get through the bumpy days by knowing God goes through them with you.

334. Reduce your stress.

335. Make sure you are compensated fairly for your work.

336. Give your willfulness a rest.

337. Be physically and emotionally available for your loved ones.

338. Before you do something you know is wrong,
     think about how you'll feel tomorrow.

339. While time away on a porch swing.

340. Enjoy a healthy sexual relationship.

341. Maintain your sense of integrity in all your daily affairs.

THE FEEL GOOD BOOK

342. Refrain from chronic caretaking.

343. At the movies eat popcorn instead of candy.

344. Be assertive.

345. Remember that you *can* go home again,
but you don't have to if you don't want to.

346. Know the difference between dreams and reality.

347. Never sell yourself short.

348. Look at the amusing side of life.

1001 WAYS TO BE HAPPY

349. In the process of helping others,
don't forget to help yourself.

350. Always trust your inner voice.

351. Pace yourself instead of trying to do everything at once.

352. Worry less and take action more.

353. Play first; work later.

354. Let go of other people's opinions and be your own person.

355. Tell yourself that you deserve the best of everything.

THE FEEL GOOD BOOK

356. Listen to the sounds of leaves crunching under your feet on an autumn day.

357. Hold a child in your arms.

358. Sit up front instead of in the back.

359. Create your own reality.

360. Eat cereal instead of bacon and eggs for breakfast.

361. Make mole hills out of mountains.

362. Sing a lullaby.

363. Don't always feel you have to be at center stage; someone has to be in the cast.

364. Read a devotion or meditation book daily.

365. Reward yourself for accomplishments with positive affirmations.

366. Be willing to provide a refuge for someone who needs one.

367. Watch a bird build its nest.

368. Make sure your spiritual workout equals your physical workout.

THE FEEL GOOD BOOK

369. Get your life organized but not too organized.

370. Let your kind words diffuse someone else's sour attitude.

371. Don't let others push your buttons.

372. Look before you leap.

373. Recognize the source of your fears and their power will slip away.

374. Respect your body.

375. Make New Year's resolutions.

1001 WAYS TO BE HAPPY

376. Sleep late.

377. Look within where you already have all that you need to be happy.

378. Tip your newspaper carrier at Christmastime.

379. Refrain from the "overs": overdoing, overorganizing, overcommitting, overscheduling, overachieving, and overindulging.

380. Spot old bad habits when they try to sneak back into your life.

381. Pay attention to what loved ones have to say.

THE FEELGOOD BOOK

382. Try something different at least once a week.

383. Let humor brighten your day.

384. Act on your intuition.

385. Avoid snap decisions and quick fixes.

386. Feel your heart skip a beat
at the splendor and beauty of a snowfall.

387. Look for life's greatest blessings in your greatest pain.

388. Don't be a chameleon in your relationships.

1001 WAYS TO BE HAPPY

389. Give your child a slingshot instead of a shotgun.

390. Use your tongue to uplift instead of tear down.

391. Put your spirituality at the top of your list.

392. Avoid whining.

393. Distinguish between standing up for yourself and depriving others of their rights.

394. Welcome change, even when you didn't ask for it.

395. When treed by a bear, enjoy the view.

THE FEEL GOOD BOOK

396. Reclaim the power in your life
that you have left to chance.

397. Don't settle for the way things used to be.

398. Make the best out of what you have.

399. Ride a carousel.

400. Drink juice instead of alcohol.

401. Have faith in something or someone.

402. Put your troubles in God's hands.

403. Find harmony within yourself first
before you try to find it in the world.

404. Express glee!

405. Avoid procrastination.

406. Listen to what your dreams tell you when you are sleeping.

407. Pay attention to your Freudian slips.

408. Wear your hair to suit yourself, not someone else.

409. Do something creative or artistic.

THE FEEL GOOD BOOK

410. Lower your standards.

411. Put a fence around the cliff
instead of an ambulance in the valley below.

412. Don't preach.

413. If you do preach, practice what you preach.

414. Never be cruel to an animal.

415. Develop your own conscience and values.

416. Don't make little things more than they really are.

417. Notice what you feel as you flip through pictures in an old family album.

418. Be a care*giver* instead of a care*taker*.

419. Let go of envy.

420. Learn from your body's memory, it never forgets anything.

421. Read the newspaper every day.

422. Have a favorite color.

423. Be willing to bend in the wind like tropical palms.

THE FEELGOOD BOOK

424. Create your mood by acting "as if" when you're down and you want to be up.

425. Be sympathetic to those less fortunate than you.

426. Eat homemade food instead of fast food.

427. Set aside one soothing moment just for yourself each day.

428. Sit in a children's swing.

429. Let go of the urge to fix someone else.

430. Avoid pettiness and triviality.

431. Add laughter to your arsenal against illness.

432. Be flexible; even a tree bends when wind blows over it.

433. Learn to *act* with the gift of human reasoning instead of *react*ing like a rat in a maze.

434. Don't shame other people.

435. See your inner beauty.

436. Have the courage to receive as well as to give.

437. Remind yourself that life is how you see it.

THE FEEL GOOD BOOK

438. Make sure you intuit as much as you analyze.

439. Offer a comforting embrace to someone who is hurting.

440. Set limits with spending money.

441. Boycott businesses that encourage prejudice to people or harm to the environment.

442. Talk, trust, and feel.

443. Memorize the beauty of a flower.

444. When you get an attitude, think gratitude.

445. Pay attention to the simple things around you that you take for granted.

446. Treasure relationships with people who let you disagree with them.

447. Always trust your inner voice.

448. Live your life instead of just surviving it.

449. See how all the "bad" things in your life have strengthened you in some way.

450. Daydream once in awhile.

THE FEEL GOOD BOOK

451. Never tell others (or yourself) that they shouldn't feel a certain way.

452. Live so that you never have any regrets.

453. Get involved in something.

454. When you think about how far you have to go, look back at how far you have come.

455. March to the beat of your own drum.

456. Notice what you're teaching to someone else, because that's the lesson you need to learn.

1001 WAYS TO BE HAPPY

457. Make your fears sit beside you
instead of letting them hover over you.

458. Don't be afraid to go out on a limb
to get to the fruit on the tree.

459. Remind yourself that success comes in can's, not cannot's.

460. Stop making "to do" lists.

461. Change the way you've always done something.

462. Look upon your life as a downhill slide
instead of an uphill battle.

THE FEEL GOOD BOOK

463. Buy only what you can pay cash for.

464. Accept compliments as the truth about yourself.

465. Manage a bad mood with a great belly laugh.

466. Understand that people are doing the best they can
with their current knowledge and circumstances.

467. Never say never.

468. Tell your family secrets to someone you trust.

469. Don't depend on external conditions for your happiness.

470. Learn to laugh at yourself in a kind way.

471. Take the time to work a puzzle.

472. Admit to God the exact nature of your wrongs.

473. Look at life as an adventure instead of as a struggle.

474. Take a deep breath before you speak to a group.

475. Celebrate the rituals, birthdays, and anniversaries in your life with vigor and enthusiasm.

476. Follow through on your commitments.

THE FEEL GOOD BOOK

477. Ask for guidance when you need it.

478. When your back is against the wall, lean on it and relax.

479. Learn to accept authority
as long as it is legal and ethical.

480. Fill up your inner holes with something spiritual.

481. Prioritize.

482. Don't be a know-it-all.

483. Do one thing at a time.

484. Don't let the wear and tear of daily living erode your spirits.

485. Fill your mind with healthy thoughts.

486. See the hour glass as half full, not half empty.

487. Have the courage to swallow your pride.

488. Learn to surrender to life and you'll be propelled forward.

489. Don't pretend to be something you're not.

490. Play a kazoo.

THE FEELGOOD BOOK

491. Remember that "guru" is spelled "Gee-You-Are-You."

492. Only make promises you can keep.

493. Acknowledge all the good things about yourself.

494. If you swallow your pride,
don't throw it up in someone else's face.

495. Curb your appetite.

496. Put your problems in perspective.

497. Be fair, not punitive.

498. Know people's nicknames.

499. Obey the law.

500. Get used to quiet in place of chaos.

501. Respect the customs of other cultures.

502. Strive for balance and moderation.

503. Don't try to appease everyone. It will whittle you down until there's nothing left of you.

504. Avoid operating in extremes.

THE FEELGOOD BOOK

505. Face controversy.

506. Push to have laws changed that are unjust.

507. Use laughter to dispel bad moods.

508. When you make fun of or criticize someone else, remember that you see in them something that you don't like about yourself.

509. Don't confuse your opinion with fact.

510. Know that admiring other people's beauty and wisdom doesn't diminish your own.

1001 WAYS TO BE HAPPY

511. Give yourself equal time.

512. Apologize when you need to.

513. Don't "throw in the towel" when you hit a snag.

514. Never think of yourself as helpless.

515. Honor other people's beliefs and lifestyles, even when they don't match yours.

516. Stop rushing.

517. Let go and let God.

THE FEEL GOOD BOOK

518. Separate yourself from self-ridicule *and* false pride.

519. Put everything you've got into your yawns.

520. Avoid magnifying your problems bigger than they really are.

521. Be aware that when you say yes to everything,
you are not choosing freely.

522. Keep your mind in good shape.

523. Find something besides the weather to talk to strangers about.

524. Be a nature lover.

525. Live by the adage, "Less is more."

526. Keep your body in good shape.

527. Refrain from leaning on your horn
when caught in a traffic jam.

528. When caught in a traffic jam, read this book.

529. Watch butterflies play tag in the sunlight.

530. Sit through a boring meeting without tapping your nails.

531. Give your ego a rest.

THE FEEL GOOD BOOK

532. Soak in a warm bath.

533. Be a kid again.

534. Don't burn your bridges behind you;
you might need to cross them again.

535. Scratch someone else's back even if they don't scratch yours.

536. Hold your head high.

537. Remind yourself that geographic escape takes you nowhere.

538. Obey the law even when a cop isn't around.

539. Avoid shortcuts to happiness;
they may take you down the wrong street.

540. Welcome the unknown with open arms.

541. Love your gray.

542. Share your experience.

543. Be aware of your fat and cholesterol intake.

544. Treat others as you would like to be treated.

545. Look for bargains, but don't be cheap.

THE FEEL GOOD BOOK

546. Share your strength.

547. Find out the source of a pain before taking a pill for it.

548. Don't force your spiritual beliefs on others.

549. Every now and then, spend a whole day
without looking at your calendar.

550. Do something adventurous.

551. Be someone's cheerleader.

552. Kid around.

553. Look for the silver lining.

554. Share your hope.

555. Keep one foot in the trenches
when the other is in the ivory tower.

556. Do what you feel inside is right.

557. Fly a flag.

558. Avoid trying to prove yourself.

559. Turn the other cheek.

THE FEEL GOOD BOOK

560. Look for the light at the end of the tunnel.

561. Be on the cutting edge, but don't go over the edge.

562. Catch children being good.

563. Put principles before personalities.

564. Drop the phrases "I told you so" and "I was right" from your vocabulary.

565. Be the first to make up after a quarrel.

566. Learn to tell a joke.

1001 WAYS TO BE HAPPY

567. Stand a little rain if you want to see a rainbow.

568. Learn to unwind.

569. Think of others.

570. Learn to be by yourself.

571. Give the same respect to a janitor
you would give to a rocket scientist.

572. Don't snack between meals.

573. If you want to change someone, change yourself.

THE FEEL GOOD BOOK

574. Avoid snap decisions.

575. Ask "What's right?" instead of "What's wrong?"

576. Live by the philosophy that "hoarding keeps you poor and giving makes you rich."

577. Dress to suit yourself.

578. Tell the truth.

579. Turn off the television.

580. Set goals and strive for them.

581. Learn to face the consequences.

582. Call it as you see it.

583. Avoid using big words that shut people out.

584. Just watch.

585. Sit in a library, smell the books, and hear the quiet.

586. If you're running on empty,
fill yourself up with something spiritual.

587. Don't be an alarmist.

THE FEEL GOOD BOOK

588. Look for beauty in the ordinary.

589. Pick a four-leaf clover.

590. Know when to get in the game and when to stay on the sidelines.

591. Avoid personality assassinations.

592. Don't point your finger.

593. Contemplate your life.

594. Let your feelings out.

595. Say something uplifting to one who is hanging his head.

596. Call people by their preferred names.

597. Simplify your life.

598. Look at people and places as if you are seeing them for the first time.

599. Take a deep breath.

600. Never equate money with personal happiness.

601. Take vitamins.

THE FEEL GOOD BOOK

602. Learn as much as you can about your family tree.

603. Be an advocate for human rights.

604. Give others the space to have their own beliefs,
even when they don't agree with yours.

605. Always know what you're eating and *what's eating you.*

606. Go fishing.

607. Maintain your sense of self in intimate relationships.

608. Avoid taking other people's inventory.

609. Vote.

610. Be a crusader for love and harmony.

611. Don't make everything a major production.

612. Dress for comfort.

613. Avoid sulking.

614. Recognition and profit are good,
     but don't let them be your only motivation.

615. Give yourself pep talks when facing a challenge.

THE FEEL GOOD BOOK

616. Create your own recipes.

617. Do something for others because you want to.

618. If there's a gulf between you and someone you care about, be the first to start building the bridge.

619. Never snap your fingers at someone else.

620. Arrange your life instead of your spice rack.

621. Set a good example.

622. Take the road less traveled.

1001 WAYS TO BE HAPPY

623. Hunt for seashells.

624. If you don't know what the word "catharsis" means, look it up and then have one.

625. Don't feel uneasy.

626. Let yourself cry when you feel sad.

627. Leave off the "white poisons" like salt, sugar, and white flour.

628. Be sassy without being rude.

629. Don't covet.

THE FEEL GOOD BOOK

630. Settle your differences.

631. Get high on life.

632. Recreate your life every day.

633. Keep a pair of thick, warm socks for cold winter nights.

634. Don't take work on vacations.

635. See the acceptance of your human limitations as a strength rather than as a weakness.

636. Meet your deadlines.

637. Pretend you're the rain when watering your garden.

638. Watch children play.

639. Know the meaning of "sour grapes."

640. When you feel hostile or short tempered, look inside for what is bothering you.

641. Eat ripened fruit.

642. Grin and bear it.

643. Do something to get your endorphins pumping.

THE FEEL GOOD BOOK

644. If you're going to slide down the bannister of life,
be prepared for some splinters.

645. Go to a park and feed the birds.

646. Don't kick the dog when you're mad at someone else.

647. Listen to and trust your inner wisdom.

648. Quiet your mind through silent prayer.

649. Turn setbacks into challenges.

650. Throw a party instead of a fit.

651. Care enough about yourself to set limits.

652. Recognize and affirm both the masculine and feminine parts of yourself.

653. Spend a day at a museum.

654. Replace "stinking thinking" with positive thinking.

655. Let your uniqueness out.

656. Accept challenges.

657. Express love through your actions.

THE FEEL GOOD BOOK

658. Visualize what you want to create in your life.

659. Open your heart.

660. If you have chosen misery for the first part of your life, choose happiness for the next half.

661. Purposely do something less than perfect.

662. Give yourself permission to kick up your heels.

663. Respect yourself.

664. See the world as a friendly place.

665. Spend time in ways that promote your highest good.

666. Discover your purpose in life.

667. Think about how you want to spend your time and energy.

668. Do the best you can with what you have.

669. Contact a friend you haven't heard from in a long time.

670. Don't always do what you're told, unless it feels right in your heart.

671. Listen to your unconscious mind.

THE FEEL GOOD BOOK

672. Make a list of all the people in your life you appreciate.

673. Congratulate someone on a job well done.

674. Remember someone's birthday or anniversary.

675. Choose being happy over being right.

676. Avoid adding insult to injury.

677. Remind yourself that happiness comes with willpower, not "won't power."

678. Ask God to remove your shortcomings.

679. Carve a jack-o'-lantern.

680. Turn fear into adventure.

681. Think prosperity and abundance.

682. Use good manners.

683. Put effort, not struggle (effort laced with negative feelings), into your life.

684. Be willing to talk about death.

685. Enjoy the process, as well as the product.

THE FEEL GOOD BOOK

686. Be a stabilizing force for someone else.

687. Dare to be different.

688. Sit with a friend who is grieving and just listen.

689. Learn the difference between self-will and God's will.

690. Prevent spiritual bankruptcy by making sure your emotional deposits equal your withdrawals.

691. When you come to a dead end, turn up another street.

692. Give openly and freely from your heart.

1001 WAYS TO BE HAPPY

693. Search for the middle ground in all things.

694. Take your own advice.

695. Learn to accept constructive criticism.

696. Trust yourself.

697. Go to a parade.

698. Make sure your mind, body, and spirit are working together in harmony.

699. Downsize without downgrading.

THE FEEL GOOD BOOK

700. Do whatever you want to do now, not tomorrow.

701. If you're on the fast track, don't mow others down.

702. Accept life instead of looking for loopholes.

703. When in doubt, give yourself pep talks.

704. Ask yourself whether you're afraid of dying or afraid of living.

705. When you're practicing forgiveness, don't forget yourself.

706. Turn a deaf ear to gossip.

1001 WAYS TO BE HAPPY

707. Daydream.

708. Don't be so hard on yourself;
this is the first time you've done life.

709. Look through a kaleidoscope.

710. Occupy yourself with living life, not just talking about it.

711. Don't eat standing up.

712. Fall head over heels in love with life.

713. Cushion your work schedule with breaks.

THE FEEL GOOD BOOK

714. Don't get on someone else's roller coaster.

715. Find one thing in life that brings you enjoyment.

716. Avoid extremes and take the middle road.

717. Go white-water rafting.

718. Remind yourself that you are the only person who can "make" you feel anything.

719. Do things that bring you stability.

720. Protect life that is weaker than you are.

721. Train your mind to think positively.

722. When someone makes you mad, forgive them and let the anger go.

723. Turn boredom into excitement.

724. Be polite.

725. Take naps.

726. When you turn a problem over to God, let Him handle it.

727. Turn pessimism into optimism.

THE FEELGOOD BOOK

728. Allow your heart to flip flop at the beauty of a rainbow.

729. Don't take things too far.

730. Take the experiences that beat you down and turn them into experiences that build you up.

731. Be kind, direct, and honest in what you say and do.

732. Get out of your rut.

733. Don't work and eat lunch at the same time.

734. Take care of your animals.

735. Don't put off until tomorrow doing what you want because tomorrow never comes.

736. Be sincere.

737. Remember: Today is the only day you have.

738. Don't work through your lunch hours.

739. Make the second half of your life better than the first.

740. Speak to yourself in a loving manner.

741. Throw back your shoulders and look the world in the face.

THE FEEL GOOD BOOK

742. Empty your mind of all limitations.

743. When you're drowning in a sea of chaos, keep a firm grip on your faithline.

744. Don't compare yourself with anyone else.

745. Make restitution where needed.

746. Spread the message of hope.

747. Build yourself up.

748. Be loyal to at least one other person.

749. No matter how bad your voice, sing in the shower.

750. Come home to yourself and you'll never be alone.

751. Live one day at a time.

752. Seek no credit for the good things you do.

753. Stop for children at a crosswalk out of kindness,
     not just because it's the law.

754. Send loving thoughts to people who ruffle your feathers.

755. Light a scented candle.

THE FEEL GOOD BOOK

756. Join life instead of waiting to be drafted.

757. Turn your weaknesses into your greatest assets.

758. Believe it and *then* you'll see it.

759. Point out the good qualities in other people.

760. Strive for peace of mind.

761. Don't give the little things that bug you
equal weight with the important things in life.

762. Never try to dominate another person.

763. Admit your faults openly and try to correct them.

764. Have a constructive outlet for your frustrations.

765. Think less about the pleasures of the moment and more about the consequences.

766. Face each day with peace, hope, and love.

767. Look for a gradual and continual change in yourself.

768. Never allow someone else to dominate you.

769. Face life instead of running from it.

THE FEEL GOOD BOOK

770. Get the things that are troubling you out in the open.

771. If you can't pronounce what the package says, don't eat it.

772. Hear the voice of God through the words of others.

773. Get rid of what you don't want in your life
in order to make room for what you do want.

774. When you feel unlovable, love yourself.

775. Stand up and be counted.

776. Treat yourself with kindness and patience.

1001 WAYS TO BE HAPPY

777. Inventory your grudges and let them go.

778. Forgive those who have hurt you
because it benefits you more than them.

779. Know that you can handle anything.

780. Let down your guard and let your love shine through.

781. Have a party for no special reason.

782. Find something that makes you feel gung-ho!

783. Don't put someone else down to make yourself look good.

THE FEEL GOOD BOOK

784. Do your own growing.

785. Remember that when you're shaking your fist
at someone else, all your fingers are pointed at you.

786. Love people and possess things.

787. Teach children that big boys *do* cry.

788. Take charge of your life, but let God control it.

789. Expect to backslide once in awhile before
moving forward again.

790. Don't trip over your ego on your spiritual journey.

791. Don't expect someone else to do your growing for you.

792. Move to the middle of the line between self-centeredness and self-neglect.

793. Live right instead of always trying to prove that you are right.

794. Know that it's okay to feel sad as well as joyful.

795. Put positive messages to yourself on the bathroom mirror.

796. Ask yourself who or what you've been hiding from.

797. Don't be an "adrenaline junkie."

THE FEEL GOOD BOOK

798. Buy yourself something simple and nonextravagant that you've always wanted.

799. Be willing to accept everything exactly as it is, without conditions, criticisms, or likes and dislikes.

800. Find contentment within yourself.

801. Strengthen your immune system by laughing at least once a day.

802. Concentrate on health and light.

803. Accept success.

804. Don't expect to find contentment in other places.

805. Do your best; no one can ask for more.

806. Cultivate healthy relationships.

807. When someone is casting aspersions,
have the courage to cast compliments.

808. Don't let a closed fist prevent you from receiving life's gifts.

809. Keep on keeping on.

810. Let love rule your heart and life.

THE FEEL GOOD BOOK

811. When the weather forecaster predicts a 50 percent chance of rain, remind yourself that there's also a 50 percent chance that it won't rain.

812. Give to yourself before you give to others and you'll have more to give away.

813. Love yourself without being self-centered.

814. Tell someone you love them while you still can.

815. Make a list of all the things you want to do with your life.

816. Take action to achieve your desires.

817. When you feel the urge to condemn and criticize, first examine yourself.

818. Learn to value the flaws in yourself just as you would those in a diamond.

819. Say goodbye to self-will and hello to surrender.

820. Have utmost respect (instead of contempt) for the overweight person exercising in tights.

821. Have a hobby or favorite pastime.

822. Judge no one.

THE FEEL GOOD BOOK

823. Refrain from packing your life too full
of activities and projects.

824. When you don't know where you're going, ask for help.

825. Don't magnify trivial disappointments and petty
annoyances into more than they are.

826. When you fall down, pick yourself up, brush yourself off,
and keep going.

827. Stay away from "meet" markets.

828. Wait for guidance.

829. Learn to get along with yourself and you won't waste time searching for happiness in someone else.

830. Pull together instead of tearing apart.

831. Let your recipe for life be equal parts joy and sorrow, love and anger, self and selflessness.

832. Remind yourself often that life is an inside job.

833. Be a people watcher instead of a people pleaser.

834. Look for messages from God on the faces of people you meet each day.

THE FEEL GOOD BOOK

835. Waste not, want not.

836. Maintain a tranquil mind.

837. When you have a spiritual awakening, tell others about it.

838. Learn to *use* what happens to you
instead of trying to *control* what happens to you.

839. Don't feel sorry for yourself.

840. Be on time.

841. Face today's problems one at a time.

842. Don't make one person the source of your happiness or sorrow.

843. See your fellow human beings as striving toward God even when they do not appear to be doing so.

844. Never try to tackle all your problems at once.

845. When you make a mistake, admit it.

846. Put your problems in a larger picture, and they will become smaller.

847. Look inside yourself for help instead of outside.

THE FEEL GOOD BOOK

848. Embrace both the hardness *and* softness that is you, because together they make you whole.

849. Quit looking for a cookbook on life and invent your own recipe for living.

850. Know people's names, especially when they know yours.

851. Watch a flower slowly open its petals and reveal its colors.

852. Do something that gives you a warm glow inside.

853. Find the Big Dipper.

1001 WAYS TO BE HAPPY

854. Remember, when things don't happen
the way you want them to, a better way is being planned.

855. Wait for a door to be unlocked
instead of trying to break it down.

856. Don't look over your shoulder at past disappointments.

857. Discipline your body and mind
instead of letting them do exactly as they want.

858. Be true to yourself.

859. Persist in your goals.

THE FEEL GOOD BOOK

860. Be able to play football on the lawn *and* pick a delicate flower for your loved one.

861. Find the Little Dipper.

862. Let the world know you are available by putting yourself "out there."

863. Look for the universal human bond that connects you with everyone else in the world.

864. Know when to step *in* and when to step *out*.

865. Decorate with balloons.

866. Notice how you are more alike than different from other people.

867. Express your feelings caringly with conviction and honesty.

868. Think about the amount of energy you spend carrying anger around compared to the relief of letting it go.

869. Remember that you grow the most in the face of your greatest obstacles.

870. Cheer up someone who needs it.

871. Never manipulate others.

THE FEEL GOOD BOOK

872. Say what your needs are instead of making people guess.

873. Add positive people to your life.

874. Live each day as if every day is a new day.

875. Make a funny face at someone while driving home from work.

876. Never use sex to prove your self-worth.

877. Believe that you are likeable and lovable.

878. Act consistently with your thoughts and feelings
no matter how your relationships swing and sway.

879. Send yourself uplifting and positive messages.

880. Don't jump to conclusions.

881. Be the master of your fate and the captain of your soul.

882. Be sensitive to other people's feelings.

883. Remember fully and forgive anyway.

884. Teach others how to treat you
by the way you treat yourself.

885. Let your imagination run wild.

THE FEEL GOOD BOOK

886. Be grateful for who you are because no one else will ever look through your eyes, feel with your heart, or touch with your hands.

887. Release any beliefs that have outlived their usefulness.

888. Never build a wall around yourself.

889. Let your world be a reflection of what you believe.

890. Don't expect people to read your mind.

891. Perform a selfless service without need for approval or appreciation.

1001 WAYS TO BE HAPPY

892. Get rid of self-destructive ideas.

893. Resist the urge to tell others what they need.

894. Own your feelings.

895. Look for meaning in your struggles and use them to your advantage.

896. Give freely to others with no strings attached.

897. Ask God to remove your "holier than thou" attitudes.

898. Give yourself permission to be who you are.

THE FEEL GOOD BOOK

899. Never do someone else's thinking.

900. Get in touch with your spontaneity.

901. Put your mind at ease so you can feel peaceful, think clearly, and act calmly.

902. Acknowledge your fears without making them a part of you.

903. Look for the *woman* in the moon.

904. Substitute something positive for bad habits.

905. Let go of self-doubt and embrace self-assurance.

906. Make *every* day Valentine's Day.

907. Visualize yourself succeeding and
doing well in situations *before* you are in them.

908. Tell yourself you are important.

909. Ask yourself who or what you've been hiding from.

910. Make your schedule work for you instead of you for it.

911. Don't lecture people.

912. Keep only one iron in the fire at a time.

THE FEEL GOOD BOOK

913. Get in touch with your sense of wonder and joy.

914. Tell yourself you are worth your own care and attention.

915. Don't let anyone put you into the position
of walking on eggshells.

916. Remind yourself that it is never too late to start fresh.

917. Let yourself be a new person each day.

918. Stop using other's opinions to measure your self-worth.

919. Use your own opinions to measure your self-worth.

920. Pull up the anchor of worry.

921. Let the winds of serenity fill your sails.

922. Live for today and plan for tomorrow.

923. Recognize that marvelous diversity and uniqueness within you that can never be put together in the same way again.

924. In order to receive, let go of hoarding, possessing, and gluttony.

925. Pass your love around.

THE FEEL GOOD BOOK

926. Love someone through thick and thin.

927. Learn to value and welcome your solitude
as a companion for your spiritual growth.

928. Expect to be awestruck every day,
as you experience your life through fresh eyes.

929. Learn to be happy even when things are not going your way.

930. Give your emotional engine a tune up.

931. Be old fashioned and use the mail
instead of a FAX to communicate with friends.

1001 WAYS TO BE HAPPY

932. Make self-examination a daily habit.

933. Practice overcoming your fears by walking right through them.

934. Never put your feelings on hold until
someone can catch up with you.

935. Look at all the wonder around you right now.

936. Be generous.

937. Don't brag.

938. Live by example.

THE FEEL GOOD BOOK

939. Choose your battles carefully.

940. Let go of those things that don't matter.

941. When choosing between two evils,
     choose the one you haven't tried.

942. Let something move you to tears.

943. Never label people or situations as *strange*
     just because they're different.

944. Don't put off mourning your losses
     if you can mourn them now.

945. When you bury old resentments,
don't put a marker on the site.

946. Chew gum and blow bubbles.

947. Get beyond worrying about whether people like you.

948. Avoid putting others on a pedestal,
because sooner or later they'll fall off.

949. Bowl over laughing.

950. Stop trying to *be* somebody and accept
the fact that you *are* somebody.

THE FEEL GOOD BOOK

951. Begin with what you've got.

952. Find time in your day to go within and experience the ecstasy there.

953. Don't let anyone put you on a pedestal, because sooner or later you'll fall off.

954. Watch the arrangements puffy clouds make as they roll by.

955. Take a day off just for yourself.

956. Let the chips fall where they may.

957. Seek ways to help others
     based on your own past misfortunes.

958. Accept all the things you think you "should" have done and
     didn't and all the things you did but "shouldn't" have done.

959. Remind yourself often that keeping everybody else happy
     isn't your job in life.

960. Listen to opposing viewpoints without
     losing your temper or your self-confidence.

961. Remember that as you set priorities, you're writing the
     table of contents of your life.

THE FEEL GOOD BOOK

962. Affirm your value as a human being with self-acceptance and self-love.

963. Give away all of your love and success and you get to keep them.

964. Stop "shoulding" on yourself.

965. Be on the lookout for unexpected events and conversations that will reveal solutions and answers to problems.

966. Achieve success by doing what you want to do.

967. Walk like a duck.

968. Stop trying to "fix" others
     when your own life needs attention.

969. Trust God to manage your life.

970. Stop struggling and accept your life exactly as it is.

971. Pay your taxes on time.

972. Remember that you are never alone
     because *you* are always there.

973. Know the difference between feeling sorry for someone and
     feeling compassion for them.

THE FEEL GOOD BOOK

974. Don't worry about how and when you'll surmount problems; let faith carry you around them.

975. Stop trying to impress others.

976. Fess up to the fact that your parents weren't June and Ward Cleaver.

977. Be a team player.

978. Worry about being spiritually correct, instead of politically correct.

979. Never say "it doesn't matter" when someone asks what you want.

980. Pay attention to your diet.

981. Leave gaps in your calendar
for the spontaneous and unexpected.

982. Cut back on caffeine.

983. Never look over the shoulder of the shopper in front of you
in the express line to count the grocery items.

984. Broadcast all the love and good that you have learned.

985. Learn to be comfortable living in your own skin
and seeing through your own eyes.

THE FEEL GOOD BOOK

986. Bombard yourself with positive thoughts and feelings.

987. Work smarter, not longer.

988. Think before taking action.

989. Avoid taking other people's inventory.

990. Be responsible *to* instead of responsible *for* others.

991. Make negative thoughts leave
when they overstay their welcome.

992. Don't blame your problems on the way you were brought up.

993. Don't make yourself a doormat and
no one will walk over you.

994. Give up bad habits that have outlived their usefulness.

995. Go to bed when you're sick instead of
worrying about everybody else.

996. Find *new* solutions to recurring *old* problems.

997. Give something away without expecting anything in return.

998. Take stock of your emotional baggage and unpack old feelings
that no longer serve you.

THE FEEL GOOD BOOK

999. Be persistent without being obstinate.

1000. Balance dependence with independence.

1001. Remind yourself that the simplest things in life yield the greatest dividends.

ABOUT THE AUTHOR

Bryan E. Robinson, Ph.D., is a nationally recognized author, consultant, and lecturer. He is a professor at the University of North Carolina at Charlotte. Dr. Robinson is also a family therapist in private practice.